My
Little
Poem Book

Marc Earl Montfleury

R T P

P U B L I S H I N G

ISBN: 979-8-89379-001-6

Words from the Author

I wrote this book because I was inspired by reading and writing. And I would like to encourage other people too.
My writing journey began as a punishment. My mom said to write a poem in a 1 subject 70 sheet notebook. I wrote the poem at the bakery near Berkeley Lake and got a snack there.

I will always remember how good it felt to write and share that poem. What started out as a punishment, turned into something beautiful that I could share with friends, family, and the entire world.

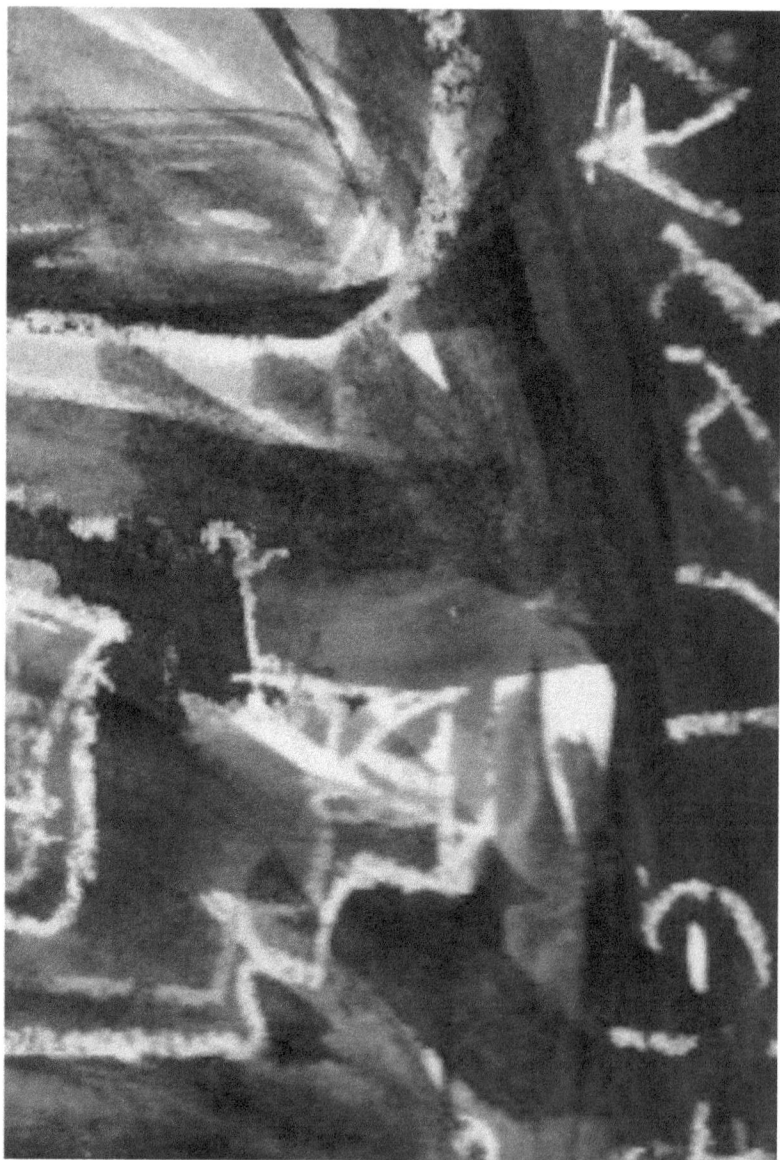

Travel Through Light

Transparent colors all around the universe.
Shining so bright
Travel. Through. Light.
What if you were faster than that? What if you were
brighter than that?
Travel. Through. Light.
In reflection, the point is really to make refraction do
it's thing
Travel. Through. Light.
The devils haunt but the point to kill them is to just,
Travel, Through, Light.
The Speed of Light is 157,000 miles per hour.
There is more to be found in the depths of space.
Bound glued, taped, tied, glued, stapled, and stuck to
space and time itself connecting together with a
special meaning.
Tunneling through the wind altar found in the oort
cloud.
The arch nemesis of spacetime is glued in a moving
expanding flat universe that's corrupted into pieces
due to alternate universes, paradox universes, and
parallel universes.
Stuck in black holes and wormholes with a big twist
of the deep deep never ending void, that contains a lot
of dimensional Rifts.
Travel. Through. Light.

HOW DO YOU IMAGINE SPACE?

My Little Poem Book

Drownwaters

Water, Rising, Drowning
Pray. Psychic, Tides Rise
Immortal, Cray.
The water rises, the water drowns.
The water rises, the water drowns.
Mortal sidekick
Sort Of Nine, Slick!
44 Oceans, Terrible Potions.
Rise, And, Rise, And, Rise To Fall!
Coordinates Crazy, Sky Turned lazy
Subtrainers, hazy
Too high. Feel the light.
The Water rises, The water Drowns.
Water, Rising, Drowning
Pray. Psychic, Tides Rise
 Immortal, Cray.
Little, Tiny, Court Game
Stay.
Water, Cluster, Many, Say.
The Water Rises
Through The Pain

Describe what if feels like

To be submerged under water

My Little Poem Book

TWILIGHT

It's a star
Chance to shine - for its whole life
Twilight, the stars, life.
Twilight, reach up to the stars
Shining light
Eclipse
So high in the sky
Come on all the life
Up high in the sky
Total bright to my eyes
Looking out the window
Too high
Total cold, shining code, come on
Worse but better in the cold night
Insulting the shining light now
Light invades all around
Just like it
Impulsing the beautiful light
Go!
All the amazing stars
Happy people
Looking. Watching.
Total bright in the sky
Beautiful constellations
High in the sky
See that?
That's a star's life
Super novas
Space discoveries
Cool light years
Drop this star
The beautiful sights in the big black sky

TWiLight 04 . 22 . 2024

Its a stars chance to shine for
its way. Like the Light the stars
Life, twilight reach up to the
stars. shining Lights eclipse.
so high in the sky. come see all the
Life, up high in the sky.
total bright to my eyes looking out
the window rooftop.
total cold shining golden on.
Worse but better in the cold night.
Inviting the shining Light now
Light invades all around. Just see it.
Impulsing the BeAutiful Light.
Galaxy the Amazing stars.
Happy people Looking. watching.
Total bright in the sky.
Beautiful constellations high in
the sky see. that? thats a star like
super novas, space discoveries, cool
Light years. drop this star, the
Beautiful sight. in the big black sky.

Write about your day

Flight Simulation

High in the sky,

All to the sun, this total mess to a whole new universe,

command a plane,

touch a space station, coordinates distract the air, that's

why there's no air in space,

all the way to the milky way, almost a light year,

Sagittarius A Star Trippin' no gravity, no light, all the way

to the atmosphere, crazy high, touch the sky,

some blue madness,

40 moons, 40 light years, peace gets disrupted,

total breeze, `

Finally, I'm in the sky.

WHERE WOULD YOU GO IF YOU COULD FLY?

My Little Poem Book

GREY SKIES

A poem of life continued
Grey Skies. Grey Skies. Grey Skies.
I wish it was blue
We're just dancing in the moonlight
Only foggy Grey Skies
Hallucinate for the country - all the geometry
Satisfying hits
OH! Take all this!
Dodge - Left - Right- All around
Moveable moments
Moments of grief
Totally not crying at CastleBerry Market
That ancient waterfall in different ways
Cascade
Seeing the removable rage
thar I got from this random man clapping at my mom
But we got free stuff so…
That's the best
Grey Skies. Grey Skies.
I wish it was blue
a cue in the moonlight
just hold tight
Enjoy your life and just relax
See
The Fun
See The Fun,
See it.

What would your home be like if you
lived in the sky?

My Little Poem Book

SCHOOL POEM

Okay

I had a bad day at school

These are not the real rules

I just don't follow them

(I just don't)

I'm just an actor

I can't control it

Buses, Peers, Scream, AHHHHHH!!!

and talk and talk and scream

That is not my inside voice

Bus 2 is just crazy

And this is why

I hate school

why do you think school
was created?

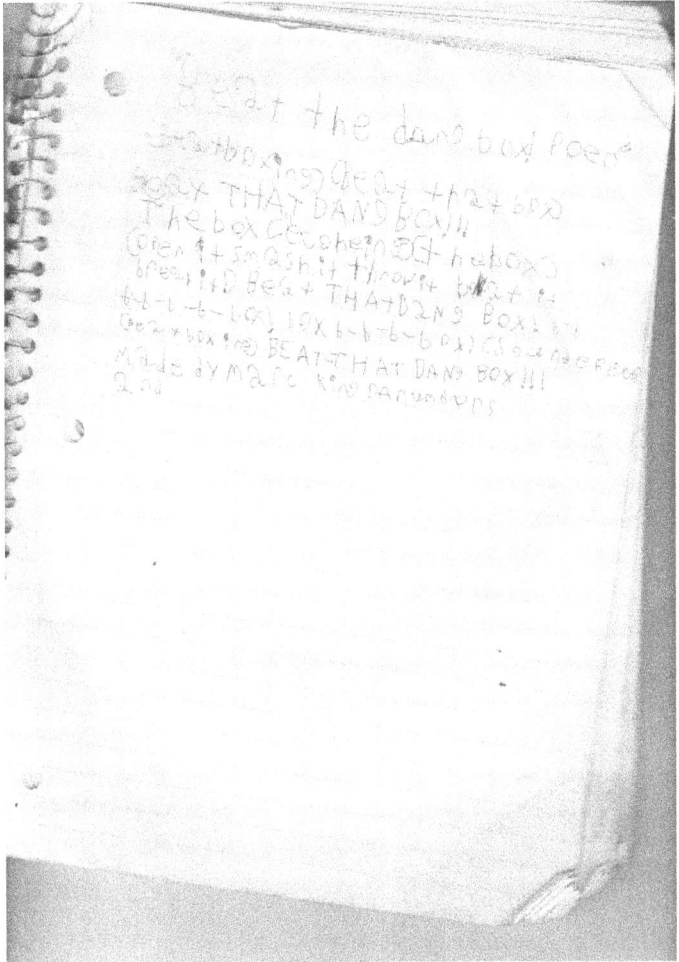

Beat the Dang Box

(Beat Boxing)

Beat that box

BEAT THAT DANG BOX!!!

The box echoing

(open it, smash it, throw it, beat it, break it)

BEAT THAT DANG BOX!!!

b-b-b-b-Box!

b–b-b-b-BOX!!!

(Sound Effects) (beat boxing)

BEAT THAT DANG BOX!!!

Write a poem using sounds

My Little POEM BOOK

GOD

God is beautiful

Shining oh so bright

Beautiful land of light

Pray to GOD

I pray for the light, All our lives

He controls our world, He created life

Here on Earth

Human Beings were created by him, his son

Jesus died on the cross

His spirit willing to heal the world

God will help you

forever and always

to this day.

WRITE ABOUT MEETING GOD

My **Little** POEM BOOK

Stress Trees

Nature and Plants

I like trees
But those big ones with branches and leaves,
I love them the most
They live in nature, my favorite element
Trees Stress
I need a rest under the trees
with some shade

Stress Trees - Stress Trees
Believe in nature
Stress Trees - Stress Trees
Believe in nature

Let the nature flow in the world
in each of us
Believe
Let the plains have many trees to grow
Believe
and the Stress goes
Bye Bye

Write about your favorite

elements in nature

Planet-ty

The Sun is blazing HOT

Mercury rumbles like solar flares

Venus burns like crazy

Earth is our home

Mafs in robot paradise

Jupiter is just a red spot

Saturn has beautiful rings

Uranus has rings with it's stinky self

Neptune has fast winds

and all the planets in all the worlds

Home to something or someone.

What is your favorite
planet? Why?

My **Little** POEM BOOK

Justice Rain

Justice
Pride
Enjoy the ride
Justice falls
waterfalls
Pride gains, Justice prays and all
Justice
Pride
Rain for the tide
Just relax
It's all you want
Just dance the track
strike the careless
take care of the homeless
Rain on justice!
Pray for the Dead
Strike the deadly
Pray for friendly
Strike the mean, clean
Pray for the Lord.
Got it, I'll soar.
After the rain,
There is beautiful grass.
A beautiful day
and trees

Be Present.

Whats happening around you?

How to be Calm

I can be calm in many different ways

Breathing, fidget toys and more.

I can relaxing during the day

Loving the pray

Loving the heathens and pains

Loving the seas and all the seasons

Searching for the course.

Exploring the darkness - Confusion of cray

Recording animals

Listening to music then watching TV

Playing my IPAD

Playing with shoestrings

Hugging my mom

Sleeping when I'm tired.

What do you feel when you are Calm?

MY Little POEM BOOK

Eclipse Attack

The total eclipse,

a shadow of things to discover.

The moon getting a big space

in the middle of the sun like it's the sun's core.

Blazing heat behind the moon like an inferno.

Shadows at the speed of light like 90 Days straight

that feels like one hour.

An eclipse.

A shadow of demons

millions of eclipses that look like a lunar eclipse in front of the earth that pours darkness all around the solar system.

Organized spaces for an lunar or solar eclipse to happen out of nowhere, on this big, rainy, day that we were about to leave new orleans, and louisiana

Go back to atlanta,

the multiple fires of sirus

a stephenson

8-12, and beetlejuice.

Always activated triggers.

Total darkness of all stars

in space

in one and only one location.

Who would want that on a rainy day?

Expand your mind, like the expansion of space.

Free Write

_____
_____
_____
_____
_____
_____
_____
_____
_____
_____
_____
_____

My **Little** Poem Book

ABOUT THE AUTHOR

Marc Earl Montfleury is ½ of the Mountain Twins. Marc and his twin sister Joyah are called the "Mountain Twins" because their last name, Montfleury, means "Mountain Flower" in French.

Born in Brooklyn, New York, to a Trinidadian mother and a Haitian father in 2017, Marc has always been interested in learning. His journey with literature began when he learned to read at only 2 years old. At 4 he created his own mini-series (with the help of his Mom), called "Counting With Junior".

Encouraged by his family, he began writing poetry to express himself. Marc also loves playing video games and swimming.